BARK, ARCHIVE, SPLINTER

JAY GAO

Out-Spoken Press
London

Published by Out-Spoken Press,
PO Box 78744, London, N11 9FG

All rights reserved © Jay Gao

The rights of Jay Gao to be identified as the author of this work have been asserted by them in accordance with section 77 of the Copyright, Designs and Patents Act 1988.

A CIP record for this title is available from the British Library. This book is in copyright. Subject to statutory exception and to provisions of relevant collective licensing agreements, no reproduction of any part may take place without the written permission of Out-Spoken Press.

First edition published 2024
ISBN: 978-1-7384125-0-1

Typeset in Helvetica Neue and Adobe Caslon
Design by Patricia Ferguson
Printed and bound by Print Resources

Out-Spoken Press is supported using public funding by
the National Lottery through Arts Council England.

BARK, ARCHIVE, SPLINTER

CONTENTS

BARK, ARCHIVE, SPLINTER   I

NOTES   33

ACKNOWLEDGEMENTS   34

They say it really doesn't hurt the tree, all that carving. But harm and hurt are different.

— C.D. Wright, from *Casting Deep Shade*

Bark, archive, splinter

There is martial time. And there is ministry of defence

The operation to manage the little commons. Hazard barracks

The need to train, to accrue one epoch. You are entering a military. Ordinance

Now, feuhold threshold dominates

Now it may not be obvious where the squadron of soldier-poets are. This could include ambushing, blank firing,
    their tenure of debrided skin

Or. Sudden noise, smoke, potential for illumination from thunder flashes, trip flares, smoke emissions, marcescent caltrops

Suspicious woody debris litter the ground like consonants. Plus wet, explosive

—————————wounded

————————————————————————vowels

Warped casings of pleasure

To contain—that is to deploy the work of carving: transformations, battle prowess, a forked toad, a crested snake, circumstances of the battle of the trees, three clashes of arms, witness the trees in battle, witness creation by maths, witness poetic prowess, adventures, more arms, and more paraphernalia, even more transformations, such boasting of arms

A marital horse

To symbolise travels then battle feats then three cataclysms then prowess then a prophetic gift

I was in a multitude of forms

Inviting duration

A hundred hosted forces. Woodmongering

Jump to today

A cavalcade of flags soldered out of imperial taffeta

Tomorrow, you arrive at the fringe of the living archive regiment: you meet alder, you meet willow, you meet
rowan, you meet knotweed, you meet blackthorn, and medlar, and rose, and raspberry, and privet, and
honeysuckle, and ivy, and cherry, and birch, and goldenrod, and pine, and ash, and elm, and hazel, and
knotweed, and dogwood, and beech, and holly, and whitethorn, and vine, and bracken, and broom, and
gorse, and heather, and oak, and pear, and clover, and knotweed, and chestnut, and birch, and oak, and
birch, and oak, and birch, and oak, and knotweed, and birch, and oak, and birch, and birch, and birch,
and birch, and oak, and birch, and oak, and oak, and oak, and birch, and knotweed, and birch, and birch,
and oak, and birch, and birch, and birch, and knotweed, and, and, and, and, and, and,   ,   ,   ,   ,

Bark, archive, splinter

Noticing the urbane saccade

A map is not the actual territory; an ideal map would contain the map of the map, then the map of that map of the map, the map of the map of the map of the

Turned into plants; tuned into deep history

See here, right inside this medieval poem, a shift or tint in diasporic style might allow the world's topography to tilt

To tinge pink

A forced opacity invisible to the untrained eye

Upscaled empire

The conference of species from militarised zones bringing supplies of conceded: wood, blood, sap, water, gold, germs, steam, breath, metal, flesh, fur, besides surplus of choric thought

Bark, archive, splinter

Notwithstanding

To save a tree from its own redacted narratology

Lucretius believed metal smelting and pottery were discovered by accident as a consequence of some forest fires

April is the smell of melting butter and chicken of the woods

Sententia

Flagged in the calorific margins of the forage

All this harvesting just to produce a commonplace for

His voiced sentences rack up as rotted sustenance or as four glade credits

Bark, archive, splinter

A dream loaned is a residency in the forest

Mountains return through the itinerary populated by figures from still life

Sent, enter, you sent for, you resent the exiled foreign poet

Wooden chalet, swapping wet shirts, usury, the sweeter possibility of staying past your allotted time in his realm

Thunder in the real life brings you out of the largesse of his whiteacre

A summer nearly spent hiking together

Where do all those lost minutes go to lay their baulk, so laden with duration

——dura

Delay, repay these tokens of grafted entwinement; whenever climate nudges you towards a boycott of its
    dog-eared lyric catalogue

————————————————————grifted

Bark, archive, splinter

Tulip path. Asphodel place

Fire danger higher today

Beasts displace the open field, an earlier picture, revolution, retardant content, a reason for listing organic forms, endlessly repetitive, he who ushers in novelty and desire, displaces the tourist's postcard

A challenge to build a glass brain

How might you sample the hypothetical. To foreground your body's fragments

Duelling branches

When does a fragment become a splinter

Defacing the melted commons

Feast and fettle

The heat, his open window, a lonely aperture, letting in vegetal grammar

Bark, archive, splinter

Where are you really from

Spinning an agrestal tale

Of gold and poison, some flight without end, the dress rehearsal, how Europa will perish, imminent destruction, the fatal illusion, a murderous rain, microbial warfare, and as for the bibliography

Land reformation

Bark, archive, splinter

Tree's tender husbandry

Ordering the elements of erasure to erect a collective or a list: blocking, clear cut, coppice, patch cut, to
pollard, to shelter wood, to strip and risk underplanting

A wish to unsend a voice message

Cicatrix, a pruned fungal shimmer

The warped paratext of shade trees

In tempering the territory of bodies foraging, erotics can be tested like steam-bent wood

I am mad about your limbs

The community at risk. Silvestral times with

Before silence, pre-history

And yet, through it all, he really was still so sensate

Bark, archive, splinter

What is the event when trees look to each other

The impulse to archive, to finger loosened wood

To make an emblem out of him

————————example

Punctuation mark, the open interval. Closeness

Turning in a surplus of resting pages, compost nodule, our transition marker

Four, five, six hours, two, three months at most

A promise to gather residual folk; gathering argent

———————————————————————————agent

Bark, archive, splinter

Operational Training Needs

There will be no penalties for anything thorn. *No wood, no empire*

Connective textus or just a paper touch: imagine a stile, a cattle grid, to survey or to sample him, imagine
pining for staffage, two men by the kissing gate, in the mire that skirts the membrane of the defence
estates, commingling civil, infected with tactical manoeuvres

Whose right to roam or to own erotic land accuses the second person

Neither safety nor security; just a fetish to reproduce infringement, tangled over the privacy of litter

Castlelaw. Danger areas imparadised by authorial paths, access points, exhibitionism

Overwriting the code for crown copyright

Bark pitch

Prove you are human, naturalised, a citizen under shade, bound by finitude

I am a tree: I regard no flesh as foreign to me

Today, the low navy risk of fire, and a clearance absent of foliar bodies

Merely an enclave of aesthetic surfeit, some porcelain deer, and a wolfish tenant

A rough draught heckling gall nuts

In the distance, a filthy war dog shakes off its vernal atoms

Bark, archive, splinter

A tree adopted by a tour for the city of the dead

Paid by the hour to enter the names of invasive species into the catalogues of

Sodden butcher paper

Punctuation, corpus, post-script, indentured bracken

On the weekends, the hanging tree walks out with your grammar whenever you open your mouth

As care comes with delay, zero compensation. And an insistence on itself

Odour of wet wood and marbled ulcers

To see liquid language in blankness, the beauty of abridgement or an interim, a video of raw lacquer purification played on loop

Psychic illness all over those restrained juniper trees

Bark, archive, splinter

You were non-native, uncommon, marginal, local, too vulnerable to twisted medieval logic

Maybe I was defenceless, unarmed

A flaw in the window's seal arouses the urge to sign the firmament with a face, a name, your drawing of a tree, the last word

The absolute minimal limits for tree-life: a central limb, a luminous halo, etymology. Putting down roots

Minutes wasted watching a heroic bee joust against the glass of a bus

The last of its noble genre

Was it wanting a way out, or a way into the skin of your thawing reflection

The desperate gulf between being drawn towards openings or towards closed captions

Anything to introduce a little doubt into this fabric's weave

To introduce herbs, bottle sedge, rushes, alder, willow, bramble, bedstraw, loosestrife, borders

To always dutifully fill in a frame; to be framed by your doubling

Assume everything can grow from illegibility

And you think, this known world, spinning past, with all its opaque bracts, could entirely fit inside the first line that will grow into a map, baroque, replete with trap streets and phantom settlements

Ghost species, how auspicious for you to have survived several of these elemental calamities

A process of refuse, allegory, motion, capture, release, before escape

Bark, archive, splinter

Once, interrupting the conversation, you asked the Director: *Why are we still labelling wineberry as invasive?*
    They've been around for more than one hundred years. They are quite useful now

Record the wind through sedentary objects that can never be pulped into pages

Like less than half of the audience laughing at a joke in a language you should have known

As you wait for the translation to arrive, delayed like lactic acid

In its adjustment to newer light and working conditions, this invasive sentence carries the plenum's cruelty,
      bruised and folioed and

Creases. The frangent land in the action of administering itself usefully

Whilst your bones cast near that tree hollow releases you from the growing loan of laughter

So how long to give a plant its green card

Bark, archive, splinter

To indurate skin

Once, at a pub in the highlands, a callused hiker enclosed you into his conversation. Misreading his adventure
jacket, you thought it spelt NEVER STOP EXPLODING. He notices your book of poetry and
confesses surprise, for. Here comes his sour breath.

Poetic language is notoriously difficult. And resists

Being opened. You repeat to yourself, you had travelled north to begin again, to clear your mind of cybernetic
riddles. And to resist being opened

To conjugate a person's stricture of feelings surrounding enchanted matter. Every second in this life you resist
      being opened

What's the matter

Love. A door opens like a bag for just a second, pre-nothing

All the tormented language in the building falls out like a glass worm in time

Parallel language speaks. It detonates

—————————————————————————denotes

As the draught robs you of your scarcity, your sound and response; not silence, no, but the noise of it

Let all the latent deictics and their heat escape

A wayward fragment, loosened from its terrible composition: *Forever is deciduous*

Outside, after a snap, the dusk leaks its atopic atmosphere over stone like an itchy resin

Everywhere, roots smuggle sound back into the earth shamefully

Except to those who die

Then. A car alarm goes off and its slick rude language gets caught on every sharp green background. In its
 interval, anxiety over a future rain spreads and spreads, over there and over there and over there and until,
 suddenly, it all stops. It's real

It's really over

Your wild spot

Bark, archive, splinter

NOTES

Parts of this poem from p1–4, including the list of trees, are inspired by the medieval Welsh poem *Cad Goddeu (The Battle of the Trees)*.

The italicised quote '*A map is not the actual territory*' comes from Alfred Korzybski's *Science and Sanity*.

'I am mad about your limbs' is from Paul Valéry's 'Dialogue of the Tree'.

'*No wood, no empire*' is a riff on the title of a wonderful book *No Wood, No Kingdom: Political Ecology in the English Atlantic* by Keith Pluymers.

'*I am a tree: I regard no flesh as foreign as me*' is an adaptation of a quote by Terence.

Part of this poem from p28–31 includes lines from Emily Dickinson's 'Summer has two Beginnings'.

ACKNOWLEDGEMENTS

Many thanks to the editors of the following places where some excerpts from this project first appeared: *mercury firs*, *Annulet*, *Ocean State Review*, *Gulf Coast*, and *theHythe*.

Jay Gao is a poet from Edinburgh, Scotland, living in New York City. His debut poetry collection *Imperium* (Carcanet, 2022) is a winner of the 2023 Michael Murphy Memorial Prize, an Eric Gregory Award and a Somerset Maugham Award. He is also the author of four poetry pamphlets and chapbooks. Currently, he reads for *Poetry* magazine and is a PhD student in English at Columbia University.

SELECTED OTHER TITLES BY OUT-SPOKEN PRESS

Boiled Owls • Azad Ashim Sharma
[...] • Fady Joudah
Vulgar Errors / Feral Subjects • Fran Lock
State of Play: Poets of East & Southeast Asian Heritage in Conversation • Eds. Eddie Tay & Jennifer Wong
Nude as Retrospect • Alex Marlow
Today Hamlet • Natalie Shapero
G&T • Oakley Flanagan
sad thing angry • Emma Jeremy
Trust Fall • William Gee
Cane, Corn & Gully • Safiya Kamaria Kinshasa
apricot • Katie O'Pray
Mother of Flip-Flops • Mukahang Limbu
Dog Woman • Helen Quah
Caviar • Sarah Fletcher
Somewhere Something is Burning • Alice Frecknall
flinch & air • Laura Jane Lee
Fetch Your Mother's Heart • Lisa Luxx
Seder • Adam Kammerling
54 Questions for the Man Who Sold a Shotgun to My Father • Joe Carrick-Varty
Lasagne • Wayne Holloway-Smith
Mutton Rolls • Arji Manuelpillai
Contains Mild Peril • Fran Lock
Epiphaneia • Richard Georges
Stage Invasion: Poetry & the Spoken Word Renaissance • Pete Bearder
The Neighbourhood • Hannah Lowe
The Games • Harry Josephine Giles
Songs My Enemy Taught Me • Joelle Taylor
To Sweeten Bitter • Raymond Antrobus
Heterogeneous, New & Selected Poems • Anthony Anaxagorou